JOANNA MURRAY-SMITH's plays have been produced in many languages, all over the world, including on the West End, Broadway and at the Royal National Theatre. Her plays include *Switzerland, Pennsylvania Avenue, Fury, Songs for Nobodies, Day One; A Hotel; Evening, The Gift, Rockabye, The Female of the Species, Ninety, Bombshells, Rapture, Nightfall, Redemption, Flame, Love Child, Atlanta, Honour* and *Angry Young Penguins*. She has also adapted *Hedda Gabler*, as well as Ingmar Bergman's *Scenes from a Marriage*, for Sir Trevor Nunn (London). Her three novels (published by Penguin/Viking) are *Truce, Judgement Rock* and *Sunnyside*. Her opera libretti include *Love in the Age of Therapy* and *The Divorce*. Joanna has also written many screenplays.

Love Child

Joanna Murray-Smith

Currency Press,
Sydney

CURRENCY PLAYS

First published in 1993 by Currency Press
in association with Playbox Theatre, Melbourne.

This revised edition first published in 1998 by Currency Press Pty Ltd,
Gadigal Land, Suite 310, 46–56 Kippax Street, Surry Hills, NSW 2010, Australia
enquiries@currency.com.au
www.currency.com.au

Reprinted 2016.

Cataloguing-in-publication data for this title is available from the National Library
of Australia website: www.nla.gov.au

Typeset by Dean Nottle for Currency Press.
Cover design by Susan Mikulic.

Cover shows Sue Ingleton as Anna and Natasha Herbert as Billie in the 1993
Playbox Production of *Love Child* (photo by Jeff Busby).

Currency Press acknowledges the Traditional Owners of the Country on which we
live and work. We pay our respects to all Aboriginal and Torres Strait Islander
Elders, past and present.

Contents

Natasha Herbert (left) as Billie and Sue Ingleton as Anna in the 1993 Playbox Theatre Centre production. (Photo: Jeff Busby)

Words Breaking Like Glass

Dorothy Hewett

We look. We know. We feel. The heart reaches out. The feet move towards each other. Slow motion rolls over us like the climate. The eyes start to search. The thunder rumbles. The rain breaks. The music swells.

(BILLIE)

This subtle note of yearning in one of the opening speeches in *Love Child* is symptomatic of the emotional tension that holds Joanna Murray-Smith's plays in a kind of precarious balance.

They are post-modern plays on a cutting edge crafted for the theatre and the audience of the nineties.

The text is feminine, subtle, intuitive, the subtext always dense and tantalising urging us on to the next revelation. At the moment of climax, words shatter like broken glass.

ANNA: You took away my peace—
BILLIE: No! No!
ANNA: I have—
BILLIE: You have—
ANNA: Nothing. Left. I have—
BILLIE: You have me. You have—

Blackout. Silence.

What then are the secrets of her craft? First the setting, counterpointed by music, is always ambiguous—one could literally be anywhere.

The stage is black: all darkness. Music playing: soulful, rich music. On the stage, two women are locked in an intense embrace. There is a surreal, almost ghostly quality to their embrace: it is timeless, placeless. Darkness. The music comes to an end and starts again.

Love Child (1993)

The Beach House. Joe's Cafe. These should be created very simply, perhaps with only one 'prop': a glimpse of sea, a neon light, or some such thing to give effect but leave the playing space free of clutter to facilitate the almost transparent dramatic shifts of mood and time.

Atlanta (1990)

While the physical settings for the scenes are suggested by the dialogue, I did not imagine *Honour* to have literal locations on the stage. The fluidity of speech, relationships and ideas in the play suggest an abstract, neutral design through which characters float…

Honour (1995)

Despite reference to photographs and the need to anchor the play in some physical space, the design should find some metaphor for Jacob's death and for his life, rather than attempt a literal setting.

Actor's note

The dialogue should be quite fast. Pauses marked or found through rehearsal should stand out as still moments in a fluid, fast stream.

Redemption (1997)

So here we are in this floating, poetic, impressionistic world which must be peopled by characters, their thoughts and their speech patterns. Like her character Billie Shields in *Love Child,* Joanna Murray-Smith is 'good with words'. Her skills with dialogue, the rhythm of her broken sentences, the build up of small self-contained scenes, contrasting with the use of soliloquy, keeps the drama moving to some sort of possible reconciliation, albeit a tentative one. It is just this tentativeness, the subtlety that is so painful and so intriguing.

The confrontation is usually between two characters in a movement like a *pavane* where they reach out towards each other, and then turn away, where their steps falter as if they were learning the dance as they went along.

She takes highly articulate middle-class characters in the post-modern world and unravels their lives for us. Interesting to compare her middle-class milieu with that of David Williamson, who, on the surface, does much the same thing. Yet one could not imagine two writers with less in common. Setting, style, dialogue, characterisation, plot and theme are all totally at odds; one playwright builds up his world realistically, the other creates her plays impressionistcally, in subtle almost secret sentences, yet it is still basically the same world seen through opposing sensibilities.

It is also interesting to speculate if Joanna Murray-Smith's particular minimalist style has come about because of the exigencies of Melbourne's Playbox Theatre where most of her plays have had their first production.

Sometimes I long for the crowded stage, the spectacular dramatic action, that sense of abundant life, even melodrama, that was once such a vital part of the Australian theatre. Maybe that is why audiences flock to the big musicals, maybe it helps to explain the continuing popularity of the opera. But what a playwright does, and the reasons for it, are no doubt multitudinous.

I have, whatever the reasons, great admiration for those who work in the difficult and restricted circumstances of today's theatre. In the intimacy of a two-hander, a four-hander, or even a six-hander, playing one character off against another can sometimes reach such a pitch of dramatic intensity it is like the snapping of a violin string in a Chekhov play. Out of the darkness of the empty stage, spotlit, stripped bare, heartbreaking in their vulnerability.

Love Child is a two-hander relying for its invention on the situation. There is little or no physical action. The tension is built up in single scenes between the two female characters. Anna, a sophisticated middle-aged woman, is apparently confronting for the first time since her birth the child she gave away for adoption when she was only seventeen. Her clothes, furniture, her lifestyle have all been constructed to do away with clutter. A survivor from the sixties, from political commitment and a failed marriage, she has constructed this cool self-contained world.

Billie is the modern young woman, ambitious, voracious for love, seemingly scornful of subterfuge, but ready to use any emotional blackmail to survive. She is like the world's orphan who can only depend on herself. The unmasking of these two women in a painful confrontation of fact and desire is the high point of the play. Both women are manipulative, both are savagely determined on their own options, until the cool detached Anna is broken open by the passionate vulnerability of Billie. The fact that the whole play is based on a lie gives it that extra frisson, the element of surprise.

Yet after all this pain and disillusionment it is Anna who makes the necessary adjustment. It is Anna who accepts without reservation the child who is not hers.

The play ends with Anna's soliloquy, moving into a counterpointed dialogue not between the two women, but each with themselves. The final lines are given to Anna:

> *And sweetly, so softly, we weep together for all the problems and the grief. And later, we go to the movies…*

So cunning the placing of that last little undercut line 'and later we go to the movies…'.

> *We look. We know. We feel. The heart reaches out. The feet move towards each other. Slow motion rolls over us like the climate. The eyes start to search. The thunder rumbles. The rain breaks. The music swells.*

Sydney
February 1998

The Need to be Loved

Joanna Murray-Smith

Love Child sprang from my desire to write a play about the need to be loved, and how that need may flow over the rational boundaries of thought or behaviour. It is, in a sense, about how the interior world sometimes dominates our exterior world. The need to love and to be loved cause a mother and daughter to face the truth about themselves and in so doing, they free themselves of their sorrow and madness. To begin with, both are fractured, incomplete women. By the end, each has helped the other to complete themselves. Love, it seems, belongs not only to conventional relationships, to blood ties, but to the strange, sometimes bizarre connections between human beings.

From a stylistic point of view, I was interested in whether I could write a full-length two-hander in (almost) real time and keep the necessary tension alive throughout. No tricks, no leaps, no elaborate scene changes. I wanted the simplicity of these two women on stage, each trapped by both their personal stories and by, to some extent, the limitations of perspective of their generation. Billie, the daughter, has taken for granted the freedoms which women like Anna had to fight to achieve. Anna is forced to realise that her ideology was not entirely noble in its motivations. It also served to deflect her from the implications of her personal choices, her own wilful blindness.

Looking back, I can now see in *Love Child* the freeing of my own 'voice'. The dialogue incorporates the rhythms of expression that are instinctive and peculiar to me, the same rhythms I think that I had previously tried to suppress, fearing they were too eccentric. The play was an enormous risk for me and right up until the first performance, I thought that it was destined to fail. I was shocked and exhilarated to find that audiences seemed to come alive to the play in that mysterious way which is almost impossible to analyse. Many productions later, both Australian and foreign, I am still surprised by the passionate feelings prompted by the play. Even when audiences have taken me to task for the ending, they have the energy of engagement with the work about which all playwrights dream.

Melbourne
February 1998

Sue Ingleton (left) as Anna and Natasha Herbert as Billie in the 1993 Playbox Theatre Centre production. (Photo: Jeff Busby)

Love Child was first performed by the Playbox Theatre Centre in the Beckett Theatre, at The C.U.B. Malthouse, Melbourne, on 22 June 1993 with the following cast:

ANNA	Sue Ingleton
BILLIE	Natasha Herbert

Director, Ariette Taylor
Designer, John Beckett
Lighting Designer, Phil Lethlean

CHARACTERS

ANNA, a film editor

BILLIE, a soap actress

SETTING

The play is set in Anna's designer home.

The stage is black: all darkness. Music playing: soulful, rich music. On the stage, two women are locked in an intense embrace: one older, ANNA, whose face is obscured, and one younger, BILLIE, who is visible. There is a surreal, almost ghostly quality to the embrace: it is timeless, placeless. Darkness. The music comes to the end and starts again. It is stopped, replayed, small sequences listened to over and over as if someone is playing their favourite music over to themselves with obsessional familiarity. A voice comes out of the darkness: BILLIE's voice, gaining strength as she appears alone on the stage.

BILLIE: One can always find an object provided one moves sufficiently far away from it. I can think of the strangest object, but I must know that in order to find it I must travel increasingly large distances. If something is foreseen ... that something must exist somewhere.

    Pause.

When I read this, it was as if the deepest part of me was staring up at me from the pages of a book. As if my heart and soul had been turned into print and given back to me. All my life I have thought to myself: If I can think of something, the process of having thought of it creates it.

    Pause. The music swells again, replays.

That's the music I imagine, sometimes, that I will meet her by.

    The music plays again.

ANNA: [*offstage*] Billie!
BILLIE: [*to the audience*] Do you hear that?
ANNA: [*offstage, louder*] Billie!
BILLIE: That's her.

    Pause.

We look. We know. We feel. The heart reaches out. The feet move towards each other. Slow motion rolls over us like the climate. The eyes start to search. The thunder rumbles. The rain breaks. The music swells.

ANNA: [*voiceover*] Windows on trams, in hotels, buses, through crowds. They are my eyes. I am searching. I have waited for this moment when I could look—

BILLIE: 'Hold.'

ANNA: [*voiceover*] Hold you close to—

BILLIE: 'In my arms.'

ANNA: [*voiceover*] In my arms. So clever with words. So clever with … So clever.

> *Beat.*

> So pretty.

BILLIE: Stronger.

ANNA: [*voiceover*] Beautiful.

BILLIE: Intelligent.

ANNA: [*voiceover*] So clever. So beautiful and so clever.

BILLIE: A little more gusto.

ANNA: My *bella donna*.

BILLIE: Recognition.

ANNA: [*voiceover*] I could see myself in you. I could—

BILLIE: Too obvious.

ANNA: [*voiceover*] The palest green eyes, like—

BILLIE: What? Like what?

ANNA: [*voiceover*] The bottom of the sea …

BILLIE: More idiosyncratic.

ANNA: [*voiceover*] Like eucalypts …

BILLIE: [*as if saying, 'not bad'*] Mmm.

ANNA: [*voiceover*] My pulse raced.

BILLIE: More feeling.

ANNA: [*voiceover*] My heart heaved.

BILLIE: Go on.

ANNA: You reminded me of a Botticelli rising like a—

BILLIE: Too fat.

ANNA: [*voiceover*] Like a thin Botticelli rising like a—

BILLIE: Let's keep it simple.

ANNA: [*voiceover*] So beautiful—

BILLIE: Once more.

ANNA: [*voiceover*] So beautiful and so clever.

BILLIE: Yes.

ANNA: [*voiceover*] We will be friends. We will make cumquat jam together in the kitchen and as I stir I will tell you the story of my lovers—

BILLIE: More—

ANNA: [*voiceover*] I will read you excerpts from my favourite books. I will read you paragraphs from Jane Austen and we will cry for all the—

BILLIE: Stories—

ANNA: [*voiceover*] And later I will give you my shawl, the grey green one, and tell you about your grandfather, the horse trader …

BILLIE: That's it.

ANNA: [*voiceover*] Your grandfather who traded horses.

BILLIE: And? And?

ANNA: [*voiceover*] And your Aunt Pearl who danced with Picasso on the Cap d'Antibes.

BILLIE: Mother. Do you dream of me? In the crowds who populate your dreams, do you hear me calling to you?

ANNA: [*voiceover*] I hear you.

BILLIE: Anna. Oh, Anna … Dearest Anna. My dearest Anna. Dear Anna… Dear Anna Christenson, this is your daughter speaking. Tell me this, do you dream my dreams? Do you dream at all?

ANNA: [*voiceover*] Tracing of natural parents…

BILLIE: I am contacting you …

ANNA: [*voiceover*] At the above address …

BILLIE: After consultation with the Government department—

ANNA: [*voiceover*] … Consultation with the Government department …

BILLIE: … dealing with the tracing of natural parents. I was told that I was born to you on April 3rd, 1968, at Bendigo Base Hospital. I realise this must come as—

ANNA: [*voiceover*] … I realise this must come as—

BILLIE: … something of a shock to you. I very much want to meet you. Could you think—

ANNA: [*voiceover*] … Could you think …

BILLIE: … about this and let me know at the above address? Yours sincerely, Billie Shield.

ANNA: [*voiceover*] Yours sincerely … Contacting. Consultation. Department. Dealing. Could you think about this? Could you think? Could you? Could? Yours faithfully. And a name.

BILLIE: Billie. Billie Shield.

Pause.

I was very careful. I didn't want to give anything away. I don't think that's fair. You might not want to know. You might have said no. And then, think of the torture a single piece of information might have been. 'I am quite tall with eyes the colour of expensive swimming pools.'

ANNA: [*voiceover*] Are you sparing me, or are you punishing me?

BILLIE: If I know nothing. Why should you? It's better this way.

ANNA: [*voiceover*] Billie. Billie Shield.

Blackout.

The lights come up. The stage has been very simply transformed into a large loft-like space with clean broad lines, wooden floors, angled ceiling and very sparse, very elegant conceptual furnishings. Both BILLIE *and* ANNA *are collected in the same pool of light. They turn to each other, in recognition for the first time. They stare at each other. They walk around each other in circles, staring at each other, checking each other out with tremendous intensity— as if they were inspecting a creature from another universe. They stop again and stare into each other's face. The strangeness of the moment breaks as* BILLIE *drops her small suitcase.*

BILLIE: I'm Billie.

ANNA: I'm Anna.

They embrace with almost violent tension and then after holding the embrace, they break free, stand back.

You're so beautiful.

BILLIE: I'm so nervous!

ANNA: You're on time.

BILLIE: I'm obsessive!

ANNA: Let me look at you.

She looks at her. BILLIE *stands amused and self-conscious under her gaze.*

BILLIE: You know, in the taxi, I could see you getting ready. Ready for me. For this. Smoothing your hair. Putting cups on a tray. Looking around the room. Did you do that?

ANNA: Well, yes I did.

BILLIE: Yes, I could see you. I could see you doing those things.

ANNA: [*nervously jabbering*] I would have liked to pick you up. I know a wonderful route between here and the airport and you could have saved on the cab fare.

BILLIE: Oh no. No. It was better this way.

ANNA: But cab drivers are a nightmare. A breed apart. Emotional revolutionaries, I call them. A very strong spirit of independence. But does one really want to listen?

BILLIE: I'm not—

ANNA: I always say to the operator that I simply won't take the ride if it's not clean. I won't get in.

BILLIE: This one was fine.

ANNA: [*rambling on*] I have to tell them exactly which way to go because I usually know the fastest route. I'm just good at navigating, always have been. I must drive them mad. They probably avoid me when they see me on the footpath! But really, if you're a bit of a perfectionist, it's like a religion. You can't let go of telling other people the best way to do things.

BILLIE: I can't quite believe it. Here we are.

ANNA: I can offer you just about anything. I bought every possibility. Are you hungry? Or thirsty? Let's get all that out of the way.

BILLIE: It's so strange …

ANNA: We could sit outside. There is a small garden. But the noise. And it could rain and then we'd have to move. I think we should stay here. I think that's best.

BILLIE: To be here. To see you.

ANNA: [*trying to hold on to form, maintain confidence*] And the flight, how was it?

BILLIE: Oh, are we going to do all that? All that how was your flight stuff? Oh, no, we couldn't possibly! You don't really want to do that, do you?

ANNA *is very taken aback by this refusal to play according to convention.*

ANNA: I see. Well, I—

BILLIE: If you start off that way it's just terribly difficult to stop. It's all cups of tea and early winters and before you know it you haven't said anything at all and it's too hard to start.

ANNA: Oh … well, yes, I …

BILLIE: I feel very … strange. It's like this conversation is happening through someone else's mouth and I'm just watching … That's very beautiful your outfit.

ANNA: Thank you.

BILLIE: Very Japanesy, kind of thing. That sort of cut, isn't it?

ANNA: Yes. Miyake is a genius.

BILLIE: I'd like to just sit here and stare at you. Stare and stare. In silence. For hours.

ANNA realises BILLIE is very much an unknown quantity: she must keep up with her.

ANNA: A little unnerving!

BILLIE: I feel like gulping, you know? Instead of taking little sips of you.

ANNA: I thought we could talk, have some tea. I could show you around and then—you must be tired—you could have a nap and then I'll wake you at five and—

BILLIE: I can't believe how wonderful this is. To have you here. In front of me. That we achieved this. Against everything. Against all the odds. We found each other.

ANNA: You found me.

BILLIE: Yes—but you allowed me to find you. And I just want to say this now—because, well, sometimes when you know someone better these things are harder to say and I don't want to miss the chance. But I'm so happy. Incredibly happy to have you. Just incredibly happy.

This is very uncomfortable for ANNA. She sounds embarrassingly restrained.

ANNA: And I am too. Yes. Very. It's marvellous.

BILLIE is slightly unnerved by ANNA and is straining to say something, but ANNA is doggedly sticking to chit-chat.

So. Look at you. So tall. Yes. What, five eight, taller perhaps?

BILLIE: I called out to you. Did you ever hear me?

ANNA: I'm sorry?

BILLIE: Did you hear me?

ANNA: Sorry? Just now?

BILLIE: So many times and just ordinary moments. Anywhere. Over all the years. I'd just say my little prayer to you. I said my prayer to you and I felt as if you knew. Not in your head of course. But some little nerve in your stomach would leap up and you'd feel me.

ANNA *is completely lost with this kind of talk.*

ANNA: Well. I'm not sure. Of course, you never quite— I'm not terribly spiritual. I mean, I don't even dream.

BILLIE: That's not quite— Anyway, I don't know. There's so much to say, but I don't know how to start. Perhaps we should just act as if we're strangers meeting—friends. Perhaps we should pretend that I am here … *interviewing* you. You are a … What are you?

ANNA: I work in the film industry.

BILLIE: So do I! My God!

ANNA: Well, what do you—

BILLIE: No! No. Let's talk about you first. I'm amazed—

ANNA: That's quite a coincidence—

BILLIE: It's not coincidence, it's, it's wonderful! Anyway, are you married? Who do you live with?

ANNA: I live alone.

BILLIE: [*looking around*] It's a stylish house. I always look at these houses in the glossies and wonder if the people who live in them ever feel chaotic. The rest of us live in houses with rooms because the walls hold us in. I think we take on the character of our houses, don't you think?

ANNA: I don't—

BILLIE *looks around admiringly.*

BILLIE: It's very … minimal, isn't it?

ANNA: I've tried to make my environment as pleasant as possible. I enjoy good design.

BILLIE: My place is a mess. I can never throw anything out.

ANNA: Clutter depresses me.

BILLIE: Fantastic lamp.

ANNA: It's Philippe Starck. That's Featherston.

BILLIE: That's so eccentric! Imagine calling your furniture names … I really like that. It's so personal.

ANNA: They're the designers! Philippe Starck is a very famous designer.
BILLIE: Oh!

She laughs. Beat.

I didn't imagine this. Somehow—well, I thought—

She breaks off and laughs.

I thought you'd live in a squishy little Victorian terrace with lots of shawls thrown over the furniture.
ANNA: Why did you think that?
BILLIE: I don't know. I suppose I needed to anchor you down in my head. Into something ordinary. Motherish.

She pauses.

But you're not motherish at all. You're still young. How old were you when I was—
ANNA: Seventeen.
BILLIE: I'm trying to imagine ... I'm here now, sitting opposite you. It's like walking into a situation that has a mind of its own. Like a film you're watching late at night that you slip into. Nothing to do with me. I'm just sitting here in it, trying to hang on for grim death.
ANNA: Well yes. But I do think that we can be very civilised about it.
BILLIE: Civilised?
ANNA: Yes. I mean, let's not get into primal screaming or anything. We're grown ups, that's the good thing. You're obviously very bright.
BILLIE: I beg your pardon?
ANNA: You're obviously very bright.

BILLIE *smiles.*

BILLIE: I heard you. It just sounded so nice!

ANNA *is a bit put out.*

ANNA: Why don't we just deal with the facts. Let's deal with the facts and then, well. That's somewhere to start.
BILLIE: [*lightly, whimsically*] The facts. Facts bore me.
ANNA: [*confused*] It's just that they're— Well, they're— They're *there* aren't they?
BILLIE: All right. The facts.

ANNA: What do you do?

BILLIE: [*laughs*] This is like a conversation with a lady on a bus, isn't it? You could be anyone …

Pause.

Look at me.

ANNA *looks at* BILLIE.

Look closely.

ANNA, *taken aback, looks more closely.*

Any bells going off?

ANNA: I'm sorry?

BILLIE: Remind you of someone? Think you've seen me before?

ANNA: Well obviously, I—

BILLIE: No. No, I mean recently.

ANNA: What do you mean?

BILLIE: On television?

ANNA: No. I don't think—

BILLIE: Elizabeth Worth?

ANNA: Who?

BILLIE: Heard of her?

ANNA: I don't think …

BILLIE: Elizabeth Worth!

ANNA: No. I—

BILLIE: My stage name. I'm an actress.

ANNA: Oh. An actor. My goodness. That's precarious.

BILLIE: I love that. I thrill to it.

ANNA: I had acting ambitions once. A long time ago.

BILLIE: That's the genes again!

ANNA: Did you go to university?

BILLIE: No.

ANNA: Oh.

BILLIE: I couldn't bear it. The idea of sitting around discussing the pros and cons of grunge bands. That's not me. I was always committed to being an actress.

ANNA: What kind of acting do you do?

BILLIE: Don't you watch *Supermodels*?

ANNA: No.

BILLIE: *You don't watch* Supermodels?

ANNA: No.

BILLIE: [*very disappointed*] Oh …

> *Pause.*

> [*Hoping she'll remember*] It's a soap. Set in an agency—there's a woman with red hair … It's Tuesday nights …

> *It doesn't ring any bell to* ANNA. BILLIE *perseveres, desperate for* ANNA *to remember it.*

And it's got these goofy kind of credits where the name comes towards you on the screen down a catwalk, kind of swaying like a body …

> *Still doesn't trigger anything.*

[*A little pathetically*] It's very high rating.

ANNA: [*apologetically*] I don't watch the commercials much.

BILLIE: But this is, well it's in all the television magazines and the wedding episode was just—well, it became part of the national mythology. It's huge. You must have *heard* of it.

ANNA: My friends really only watch current affairs and the odd BBC serial. We must be out of touch.

BILLIE: [*still trying to convey the significance*] I'm recognised practically *everywhere*. Even just now, on the plane …

ANNA: Well, it sounds very … interesting. I've always wondered about those shows. They sort of paralyse people into ordinariness …

BILLIE: Is that what I do?

ANNA: No, of course not. I'm being very—cynical.

BILLIE: You really need to know something about the business to realise how lucky I am. Ninety-five per cent of actors are unemployed. I have a six-month contract. By which time they will have decided if Angelique is worthy of the core soap family.

ANNA: Angelique.

BILLIE: She's a high fashion model on the surface. And under the surface she's a suburban nymphomaniac.

ANNA: How nice.

BILLIE: It's very challenging, because she has to work on two levels.

ANNA: Oh, dear!

BILLIE: I get a lot out of acting. Sometimes I can feel Angelique inside me looking out at the world and I think how wonderful to be able to see life through different histories, different feelings.

ANNA: Is she that complex?

BILLIE: Characters grow. Not in the show. Beyond the show, the characters grow inside you.

ANNA: Is that the kind of acting you want to do? I mean, where do you go from … *Supermodels*?

BILLIE: I've been offered a part on *Taxidrivettes*—that's the series about female taxi drivers who are undercover sex therapists. It's got a nudity clause.

ANNA: You have to strip off?

BILLIE: Well, it's not that bad. I mean, I am in good shape.

ANNA: But it's … well, isn't it demeaning?

BILLIE: Unemployment's demeaning!

ANNA: Doesn't it worry you what people think?

Pause.

BILLIE: What do you think?

ANNA: Well. I—

She breaks off, reluctant.

BILLIE: Most people think it's fantastic. Of course the intellectuals think it's exploitative, but they take it all more seriously than anyone else. Your average watcher knows it's cliché-ridden, morally bankrupt sedation, but they enjoy cliché-ridden, morally bankrupt sedation.

ANNA: That's one way of looking at it.

BILLIE: Look, it's not Chekhov, but what's Chekhov got to do with life? All his plays are about people who *think* about life. Most people don't think about life. And they don't have houses in the country and big tea urns or friends who are melancholy doctors.

ANNA: I think Chekhov is very contemporary.

BILLIE: [*sadly*] Here I was thinking how surprised you'd be to open the door and see Angelique on the doorstep! The joke was on me, wasn't it?— That you're the last living person who doesn't watch the show! You're not at all impressed with my success—of course you're not! You would have liked to me to go to University.

ANNA: It's not important. I had a great time there. I grew up there, that's all. I don't mean to be critical. I'm sure you're a wonderful actress. It's just that I keep wondering if things are worthy or not— and I suppose that question is rather out-dated.

BILLIE *thinks for a moment: taking in the surprise.*

BILLIE: It's so different. I thought you'd be so—

ANNA: What?

BILLIE: Nothing. It's silly.

ANNA: No. Say it.

BILLIE: Well … Proud. Something.

ANNA: I am.

BILLIE: No. No, you're annoyed.

ANNA: Not at all.

BILLIE: A two bit actress, so pleased with herself!

ANNA: Look, no. Really—

BILLIE: What a fool. To think you'd even have seen me. To think you'd hold that as some great—

ANNA: I think it's marvellous you're such a success.

BILLIE: But it means nothing to you!

ANNA: Well, it's not my thing! Soaps and all that. But that doesn't mean it's not an achievement.

BILLIE: Do you think I'm too *naive*, or too *crude* to understand I'm being patronised?

ANNA: Well, listen, I mean we don't have to *approve* of each other. That's not what it's about.

BILLIE: What *is* it about?

Beat.

Anyway, when I've got enough money, I'm going North. I'm going to buy some land near a rainforest and build a tree house and just lie around all day thinking about the earth.

ANNA: You're into the environment?

BILLIE: Yes. But I don't like talking about it much.

ANNA: But that's something to be proud of—

BILLIE: It's a private thing. You know, like a wild place you dream of and if you talk about it, it loses something.

ANNA: And is there anyone special?

BILLIE: A lover, you mean?

ANNA: Yes.

BILLIE: She's an air hostess called Kirsty.

ANNA: How … ah, *marvellous*. I've always thought it would be tremendous to be able to explore all one's—

BILLIE *laughs.*

BILLIE: I'm *joking.*

ANNA *looks taken aback.*

I had a boyfriend called Stuart but it's over. It's ...

ANNA: What happened?

BILLIE *thinks.*

BILLIE: Well he ... Oh, nothing. I don't want to— Do you mind if we don't—?

ANNA: Fine.

Pause.

What did he do?

BILLIE: He was ... weak.

ANNA: No, I mean what did he *do*?

BILLIE: Oh, he was a ... he was a doctor.

ANNA: Did he leave you?

BILLIE: Oh no. No. He was just a child, really. He had no courage. No vision. Weak. I try to make things happen and he just wants sit back and let life unfold. Forget it. We make things happen. He thought I agitated about everything, asked too many questions, doubted things that ought just to be left alone.

ANNA: Sometimes you just do what has to be done. To save yourself.

BILLIE: I don't understand.

ANNA: It takes courage to do the right thing.

BILLIE: What makes you think I did the right thing?

ANNA: Well ...

BILLIE: You don't know either of us.

ANNA: No, but—

BILLIE: I'm not at all sure that I've done the right thing.

Pause.

ANNA: Who do you live with?

BILLIE: On my own now.

ANNA: It can be very liberating to live alone. Not to pander to anyone's whims.

BILLIE: *He* pandered to *my* whims. I miss his pandering.

ANNA: There is tremendous freedom in living alone.

BILLIE: I don't find any freedom in it at all.

Pause.

Look, I didn't mean to snap at you. About Stuart, before. It's just. Well—

ANNA: That's okay.

BILLIE: It's just. Well, when you let something go, don't you keep looking over your shoulder to see if it's still there, if it's too late? When you wonder if you've done wrong for yourself?

> ANNA *says nothing.* BILLIE *allows a silence and then starts up again.*

Anyway, there's no love in my life! No back rubs for me. I just work and eat and sleep.

ANNA: Do you have interests? Book clubs? Politics?

BILLIE: What do you mean?

ANNA: Are you involved with any—causes?

BILLIE: Not really. No. Are you?

ANNA: I used to be. When I was your age.

BILLIE: What sort of causes?

ANNA: Well, it was the late sixties. Everything was changing.

BILLIE: Oh, the sixties.

> *Beat.*

Sometimes I think you really ought to be dead before you're immortalised.

> ANNA *laughs.*

ANNA: Of course later generations have had to reinvent us. Somewhat shabbily. To justify their own apathy. I look around me now and I feel sad that— Well, it was just such an amazing time. It sort of gets more and more amazing—as if it was some sort of 'enclosed' time. Sort of unto itself.

BILLIE: That was you, was it, on Parliament steps in kind of loose purple shirts and pendants?

> ANNA *thinks and reluctantly is forced to admit to the outfits.*

ANNA: Yes.

BILLIE: Don't tell me—you were fighting for the right to wear loose purple shirts and pendants in public?

> BILLIE *laughs.*

Wow—lucky for all of us you won that battle!

ANNA: I was at University and I sort of fell in with a group—and they were right at the heart of what was going on. I'd never encountered anything like them! I'll never forget the first time I saw Douglas Hatfield smoking these enormous reefers up the back of the caf. I thought he was Jim Morrison and Jean-Paul Sartre rolled into one. He—he was sort of the reason I got involved. I was such a timid thing and they were—they were so fierce! I was attracted to their—well, I don't know. They believed in justice. They believed in fighting for … Where would we be without the sixties? It's like we rose up to claim the future …

BILLIE: It's as if it had an edge around it—

ANNA: Maybe you will feel that about your time.

BILLIE: I don't think so. No one's going to write a book about *my* time. No one's going to make movie scenes with great soundtracks about my history.

ANNA: It's amazing how the myths sneak up on you. We were completely caught up in the moment. We were very active on campus. Vietnam and all that was raging. We had a conscientious objector staying with us for a month—what was his name? Fred? No, Frank. Frank. He introduced me to Patti Smith.

   BILLIE *is silently watching and listening.*

I nearly got chucked out of Uni. We barricaded the doors leading out of the Dean's office. He had to call security to get out. We'd painted his station wagon with … something. That was the night we— My God, the Rolling Stones were playing at Kooyong. I had to hitch and … I don't think I ever got there … Astrid was devising a play about patriarchal— No, no, that was another time … There were all these gorgeous women running around with all these— well, they were such drips now that I think about it! We were all on the pill and it was—it wasn't like now—it was messy, all those relationships. But I was under a spell. Parents, parents' friends, the suburbs, all those boring expectations just crashed. I had hair down to here and I wore those crushed velvet—

BILLIE: In all this time, have you … Did you imagine …

ANNA: What?

BILLIE: About *me*.

Sue Ingleton as Anna in the 1993 Playbox Theatre Centre production.
(Photo: Jeff Busby)

Beat.

ANNA: I tried not to—

BILLIE: Oh …

    Beat.

    But every once in a while. You must have—

ANNA: No.

BILLIE: Oh …

ANNA: I tried not to wonder because—it was never-ending. If I started to do that. I just felt, I would never be free. Imagine the tragedy of looking everywhere. Cafes. Post offices. Imagine always looking at people and wondering if—

BILLIE: Yes.

ANNA: I think I just tried to make things easier for myself. There didn't seem any point—

BILLIE: I see.

ANNA: Are you all right?

BILLIE: I'm … I'm surprised. I thought—

ANNA: Yes?

BILLIE: That this would be very emotional.

    Pause.

    I assumed that the emotion would just— Well, that somehow you would be—moved or something. You're looking at me. I am your daughter.

ANNA: I am moved.

    Pause.

BILLIE: Of course there's no reason to feel— You probably have a whole different way of dealing with— It's been a very difficult journey for me to get here. Right here.

ANNA: I'm sure it has.

BILLIE: I had to wait for my parents—

ANNA: They're dead?

BILLIE: Yes.

    ANNA *waits for more.* BILLIE *clearly isn't going to provide details.*

I couldn't look for you until they died. They would have been devastated. I would never have been able to argue well enough that this had to happen and that it wasn't a reflection on them.

ANNA: Are there brothers and sisters?

BILLIE: One— [*suddenly irritable*] I don't want to talk about this! This is about us.

ANNA: Oh, well. Sure. I mean, the rest can wait. We can fill these things in—

BILLIE: Anna. Can I talk to you?

>   ANNA *is very taken aback.*

ANNA: Well, of course.

BILLIE: I mean *really* talk?

ANNA: Yes.

BILLIE: About when I first started to look.

ANNA: Well, yes. Yes.

BILLIE: Can you bear it? I mean would you rather talk about—you know, nothing things?

>   ANNA *is embarrassed, unnerved again.*

ANNA: Of course not. No. Go ahead.

BILLIE: I was sixteen.

ANNA: I see. Yes. That's interesting.

BILLIE: It was one of those things that poisoned my blood, so slowly I didn't recognise it. I always denied that I wanted to know. I always said: If she doesn't want me, I don't want her.

>   *Beat.*

You.

>   *Beat.*

Isn't it funny? All the 'hers' are 'yous' now.

>   ANNA *looks at* BILLIE, *finding this terribly difficult to hear.*

Then one day I was watching a movie with a friend. Ridiculous really. A kind of Hollywood tearjerker. *Ordinary People.* Did you see it?

ANNA: No.

BILLIE: Very emotionally manipulative—the way those American films are. Well, of course they are—that's why they work. And this child in the family is in so much pain. And the actor was fantastic. Everyone was fantastic. Mary Tyler Moore was the stitched up mother who couldn't cope, couldn't love, couldn't be loved. And the child was the walking illustration of the mother's disability. And the whole thing just … shifted something in me. I felt this huge … ball, rolling inside of me and I thought well, this film isn't my story, but this mother, child, family, tragedy, feeling, unfeeling, all of it: that's me. That's this great, *grief*, inside of me.

Beat.

I waited. I knew what I had to do and that made the waiting tolerable. Just knowing that I had to find you was in itself a relief. When they died, I couldn't help it—I was about to soar …

ANNA: That's very. Well, that's very. Poignant.

Pause.

Were they good to you?

BILLIE: Sure. They were good to me.

ANNA: They were good people?

BILLIE: Yes. Why?

ANNA: Well, it's good to know that you were in good hands.

BILLIE: [*genuinely shocked*] What a strange thing to say …

ANNA: Really?

BILLIE: Well, I mean. Yes. Yes, it is.

ANNA: [*defensively*] Well, perhaps it is. I—I can understand how you might expect me to be more emotional, but there is more than one way of feeling things.

BILLIE: Really, I didn't mean anything by—

ANNA: You never knew my story.

BILLIE: Look, I *know*. I didn't mean to—

ANNA: You didn't know me. You saw everything from the point of view of the child.

BILLIE: I *am* the child.

ANNA: Quite. But there is always the other story.

BILLIE: I don't think a child sees things like that.

ANNA: We are both equipped with intellects. We can manage this.

Beat.

I'm a very emotional woman. Very. That's my weakness.

BILLIE *says nothing.*

And I'm very glad you wrote. I'm really very pleased that we can do this. Can deal with this.

BILLIE: You took a long time to—
ANNA: It wasn't that I had any doubts. It was just a matter of finding the right words. When I received your letter, I felt a huge, great, relief. I wanted to fix it up.
BILLIE: Fix it up.
ANNA: Come to terms. There's no point burying one's head in the sand to avoid—

She realises what she is saying and immediately rephrases.

Difficult experiences. We have to tackle them head on.
BILLIE: Yes.
ANNA: And my comfort is that with the passing of time you have become a clear-headed young woman and you have the ability to get some perspective on things.
BILLIE: What makes you think that?
ANNA: Of course you do. You're intelligent.
BILLIE: Why would that make any difference?
ANNA: Of course it makes a difference. If you put our situation in a context, it is much easier to understand.
BILLIE: What does context mean? I've always wanted to know.
ANNA: We have evolved, haven't we? We don't run around casting blame on people who are simply the victims of a time and place …
BILLIE: You seem to be anticipating something.
ANNA: What do you mean?
BILLIE: Blame. Is that why you think I wrote?
ANNA: I was seventeen.
BILLIE: So?
ANNA: I was very young. It was very different then. Women did what they were told. Society. The Church. Fathers. I did what I was told to do.
BILLIE: You make it sound as if it all had nothing to do with you.
ANNA: Well, yes. I mean, I was a victim of a time. I was everything that I later fought against: a woman who was made to feel powerless, will-less. I had no control. No status. Later, I spent a lot of years fighting for a world that made women feel stronger.
BILLIE: I don't know that I feel so strong.
ANNA: Compared to me, your place in society is very strong.
BILLIE: What about my place inside myself?

Beat.

ANNA: Do you want me to show you the guest room?

BILLIE: Ah … Well, do you want to do it now?

ANNA: Well, whenever.

BILLIE: Maybe, later. I just. I don't want to— Maybe, later.

ANNA: Fine.

BILLIE: Have a lot of 'guests' do you?

ANNA: No. Actually none while I've been living here.

BILLIE: I guess I'm the guest that gives the room its name, then.

ANNA: I don't like people staying much. Well, not you of course! But usually it just disrupts me.

BILLIE: Well, I'll try not to disrupt you too much.

ANNA: Oh no! Really, I'm thrilled to have you here. After all, you're my— It's quite different.

Beat.

[*Lightly*] You can stay for a while?

BILLIE: I don't know. I thought I'd just see how— I didn't want to feel that I had to rush back the moment I'd found you.

Beat.

Anyway, I don't know anything about your life. Except you live alone with a lamp called Philippe.

They laugh.

You said you worked in the film industry.

ANNA: I'm a film editor. I edit film.

BILLIE: That's an incredible job. You have a lot of power.

ANNA: Spoken like a true actor.

BILLIE *laughs.*

Did you see *Bogged Down* last week, on the ABC—the documentary on the fauna of bogs?

BILLIE: Ah, no …

ANNA: I do a lot of nature documentaries for television. You know, wildflowers and bumble-bees.

BILLIE: That's great. Of course you don't get much of a billing do you, as an editor?

ANNA: You don't get your name above the title, no.

BILLIE: So it's well paid?

ANNA: Not really. But I like it.

BILLIE: Wow …

> *Pause.*

And what about the rest of your life?

ANNA: I'm divorced.

BILLIE: What happened?

ANNA: I got married when I was twenty-five. To Edward Berg.

BILLIE: U-huh.

ANNA: You don't know him?

BILLIE: Should I?

ANNA: The writer.

BILLIE: Oh.

> ANNA *is very surprised.*

ANNA: You haven't read him?

BILLIE: Does he write well?

ANNA: Yes.

BILLIE: I don't read anything well written. I like books with titles that are raised. In gilt. That's gilt without the 'U'.

ANNA: He's a very good writer. A good writer, but not such a good person. Well, actually he is a good person. He just wasn't a good husband.

BILLIE: What was wrong with him?

ANNA: He was … He never … He couldn't communicate.

BILLIE: What does that mean?

ANNA: He never talked to me about the way he felt. Every time we spoke to each other it was about life out there. Or doing things.

BILLIE: Some people find that kind of thing hard to say. One day we'll see all this mumbo jumbo about communication as hysterical and unreasonable.

ANNA: I think there's a certain obligation to try to share your feelings in a relationship.

BILLIE: But do you have to use words? I mean, that means the people who are skilful with language always win.

ANNA: Well, perhaps but—

BILLIE: Was that the whole reason you broke up?

ANNA: We were married fifteen years. There were a lot of reasons. He took a lot of things for granted and I felt as if I was losing my identity.

She pauses, wavering.

He wanted to have children.

Beat.

BILLIE: And you didn't?

ANNA: No.

BILLIE: Why not?

ANNA: It's complicated.

BILLIE: Because of me? That's terrible. I mean, just because it didn't work when you were eighteen—

ANNA: Seventeen—

BILLIE: That doesn't mean—

ANNA: It wasn't to do with you.

BILLIE: Oh.

ANNA: I felt that having a child would disrupt everything. I was just beginning to get jobs without having to grovel for them. The phone was ringing. I was learning a lot—starting to feel that I was a good editor. I didn't want to have to drop everything to change nappies. He wouldn't have. He wanted a child, but he also wanted someone to do all the work. He was fine. He'd keep writing short stories and winning competitions and getting his face in the literary pages. While I sank deeper and deeper into suburbia.

BILLIE: Didn't you want one, though?

ANNA: I wasn't going to entertain the idea because I knew that all his high-minded promises would disintegrate. Why should I pay the price of his dishonesty?

BILLIE: Didn't you ever think about the good things?

ANNA: Oh, sure. Babies. Cute. But you know, you don't just have this beautiful little thing and pick it up and put it down when you want. It's yours for life.

Uncomfortable silence.

I mean—

BILLIE: That's fine.

Beat.

ANNA: I'd read a lot of books. I didn't want to be used as some kind of breeder. The conduit through which his ego would perpetuate into the next generation.

*Sue Ingleton (left) as Anna and Natasha Herbert as Billie in the
1993 Playbox Theatre Centre production. (Photo: Jeff Busby)*

BILLIE: U-huh.

ANNA: I didn't want to be part of the continuum of bad habits.

Beat.

BILLIE: You don't think it's natural, then, to feel a baby in your arms?

ANNA: For most women. Maybe.

BILLIE: Sometimes I think—well, I think that one day women will look back at this time and see the madness. The way we do about slavery. That a time so hell-bent on fighting nature could be so convinced of its own credibility. Don't you sometimes think that? That the easiest thing would be to have a child suckling. And we could relax into something that isn't about choice or taking control, just about biological instinct. About being womanly. And all of us—acting in soaps, editing film, whatever—we are all trapped in some elaborate fight against instincts that would really free us? There's so much defensiveness, we've forgotten how to question ourselves—it's just automatic.

She looks at ANNA.

ANNA: I think you're dangerous.

Beat.

I mean, I think that's dangerous. You can clothe it all in middle-class modern-ness but you're just a slightly hipper enemy than they used to be.

BILLIE: Enemies. Women. It's all so much safer if you write it big. What about us? You and me. Isn't that where the real stuff is happening? If we all looked at our own hearts, this rhetoric would mean so much more.

Pause. ANNA *is unnerved by* BILLIE.

So what happened to him?

ANNA: Who?

BILLIE: The famous writer I haven't read.

ANNA: He remarried. A blonde sociologist. Very smart apparently and they're very happy. I've heard he shares the domestic tasks with absolute commitment. Whistles while he Spray n' Wipes. Lucky blonde sociologist. They have two clever, beautiful children called Oscar and Grace who roam through life in Osh-Kosh overalls ...

BILLIE: Sounds good.

ANNA: I have no regrets. I'm looking forward to getting older without all that work, you know, all that work to do with loving and living together. I'm glad that there's a whole section of bookshops I don't have to go near.

BILLIE: Do your feelings always follow your principles?

ANNA: Yes.

Beat.

BILLIE: Don't you ever get lonely?

ANNA: Absolutely not. I'm looking forward to travelling into old age reading entire bodies of work by favourite writers—Dickens, George Eliot, Vita, Alice Munro—eating what I want, dressing how I want.

BILLIE: But what about—

ANNA: What? Sex?

Pause.

Sex is over-rated.

BILLIE: Well, I was going to say 'love'.

Silence.

ANNA: Oh, love. Oh, forget it. Love. I mean, what does *that* mean? Going to dinner parties with other couples and waxing lyrical about gourmet cycling trips through Tuscany? No thanks.

BILLIE: Well, there are—

ANNA: Look, I'm not into fairytales any more. Marriage. Love. It's like some sick religion for little girls and when little girls eventually grow up they get slapped in the face with reality. A world constructed to keep them in their place: right through to guilt trips about breaking free. That's guilt with a 'U'.

Beat.

How did this start?

BILLIE: Love—

ANNA: Yes, well. I don't know about love any more.

ANNA gets up and walks around, lost in thought, troubled, then breaks in very softly.

I mean if you knew then what you know now, maybe everything

would be different. We make certain choices because we are influenced by … by the icons and then well, the icons move on. They go back on what they once said. They admit they made mistakes. Which is fine for them. But for those of us who hung on their every word … Some of us might have lost something in all of that …

BILLIE *realises the pain in this woman.* ANNA *regains her sureness.*

Of course, we gained a lot too.

BILLIE: Anna, I—

ANNA: Yes.

BILLIE: Do you think you could tell me about— About when you had me?

ANNA: Oh. Yes.

BILLIE: It's just that I really do need to fill that in. These questions have been knocking around for quite a while now.

ANNA: Of course. Yes. Well, I'll stick to the facts, I think.

BILLIE: The facts, again!

ANNA: You're quite right—they never really do anything justice on their own, do they? Still, I think it would be the best way to proceed.

BILLIE *says nothing.*

I had just finished school. I was sent to England by my parents— visit the relatives, see the mother country. I went on a boat and I met a man. I thought it was all very glamorous.

Pause. As if remembering a tale she has memorised in a very particular way.

I thought it was all very glamorous, I had left school and wanted to seize life in a single gulp. Everything. Sex. Love. Mystery. Danger. And I got pregnant and when we reached Southampton, there was his lovely fiancée to meet him and off he went. By the time I got back to Australia I was five months pregnant. My mother's face as I got off the boat. I wiped most of it.

Pause.

I just wiped most of it. Swept a cloth over my memory. I know it was awful—how could it not have been awful? The cleanest solution, so far as my parents saw it, was no longer an option. It was too late. They packed me off to cousins in the country and six months later I was home as if nothing had happened. All the friends thought I'd just got back from England and the surfaces were all smooth.

BILLIE: Have you told many people this story?

ANNA: No. Why?

BILLIE: It's just so. It sounds as if you've—

She pauses.

What was his name?

ANNA: William.

BILLIE: William what?

ANNA: I can't remember.

BILLIE: Was he Australian?

ANNA: English.

BILLIE: Well, what was he like?

ANNA pauses, trying to remember.

ANNA: He was… Well, he was tall. Tallish. He was older than me, by a few years. He was. Well, he was. I don't remember.

BILLIE: Was he dark or fair or what?

ANNA: I think he was … I think. He was fair … I think.

BILLIE: Did you tell him?

ANNA: We didn't exchange addresses. There was no point. It would have been unnecessarily complicated.

BILLIE: Do I look like him?

ANNA: I don't remember.

BILLIE thinks, gets up, walks around the room, getting tenser, feeling building.

BILLIE: Can you try and remember?

ANNA: I can't remember.

Pause.

I can't remember.

BILLIE—still moving.

BILLIE: Did you feel anything? Did you feel anything about him?

ANNA: No. He— It was just—

BILLIE: It didn't mean anything.

ANNA: Look, I was seventeen. It was … It was sex.

BILLIE: Well, I hope he was a good fuck, at least.

> BILLIE *stares at her*—ANNA *is caught in her stare. There is a new tone in* BILLIE*'s voice—an edge building that is less genial than before, less calm.*

It's little strange, don't you think?

ANNA: I'm sorry?

BILLIE: Look at me! *Flesh.* Look at the shade of my skin and the way I wear my hair. Here. Like this. The angle that I turn my head when I listen. Do you see? Do you see? You throw me these pathetic memories. I was *made* from these memories. They *are* me.

ANNA: Look, I'm afraid I just can't make more of it than it was. It seems incredible that something so unspiritual could result in a ... in a woman, I know, but—

BILLIE: A few weeks earlier and you would have had an abortion?

> ANNA *pauses, it's difficult but she must be honest.*

ANNA: Yes.

> *Silence as* BILLIE *takes this in.*

BILLIE: Is it better to have no story to tell at all than a difficult one, do you think?

ANNA: That's an impossible road to travel down.

BILLIE: Didn't you ever think that you might keep me?

ANNA: [*says nothing, then*] No—

BILLIE: Well, why not?

ANNA: Do you really want to—

BILLIE: Yes. Yes I do.

> *Beat.*

ANNA: From the very beginning, it was something that was never going to happen. From the moment my parents knew, the issue was of— making it go away. There was never any time to think of anything else—

BILLIE: There was nine months.

ANNA: The whole time was like waiting to switch something off. The idea of just going with this—

BILLIE: This—

ANNA: This pregnancy.

BILLIE: This child.

ANNA: Well yes. All right.

BILLIE: Me.

ANNA: Look, it doesn't help— If you could just hold off on doing that. Saying 'Me' like that. I'm trying to say it as it happened. Not from you. Not about you. It's not about you.

BILLIE: But it is!

ANNA: Well, yes. Of course. In the end. But *then*—it wasn't about you as you are now. Sitting here in front of me. Can't you see that? I can't tell it from the point of retrospect. From the future looking back. It's a story that can't be told except from inside it.

BILLIE: My whole life has been inside it.

> *Beat.*

There must have been a time when you wondered—

ANNA: I didn't wonder.

BILLIE: But it was a choice.

ANNA: I didn't wonder.

BILLIE: You must have thought about it.

ANNA: It didn't feel like a choice. Having a child. The child. Was just not entertained. My whole understanding of giving birth was of finally reaching a point when I could go back to where I was. Only, of course, you can never go back to what you were.

BILLIE: You did your best.

ANNA: I guess I did.

> BILLIE *says nothing.*

Do you really want to talk about this? Is this why we're here?

BILLIE: I'm interested that you never even thought about holding on to your child. I'm interested in your amazing generosity to society.

> ANNA *cannot let this go.*

ANNA: [*gently beginning to fight back*] Do you think acting in a soap opera is making any kind of contribution? Doesn't it occur to you that playing a nymphomaniac is not exactly a brilliant contribution for improving the status of women?

BILLIE: I hate to break it to you, but there are people out there who don't rush home to watch the latest documentary on the mating habits of insects. Tell me, do you just edit out the bits of animal

behaviour which aren't ideologically sound? I'm *famous*.
I get fan mail. I'm at the cutting edge of this industry!
ANNA: You're sending out a dangerous message that it's all right to laugh at the degradation of women. Do you think that's all right?
BILLIE: It doesn't really bother me.
ANNA: Does *anything* really bother you?
BILLIE: Do *I* bother *you*?
ANNA: My God—you wear your ignorance like a medal! You don't understand what we won for you. Women like me. You know *nothing* about your history.
BILLIE: Which history are you referring to? You're so judgemental about the future when the future is exactly what you were beckoning in.
ANNA: I didn't beckon it in.
BILLIE: No. You gave it away.

> *Beat.*

ANNA: I think we should get back to the reason you are here. This is just—abstract. It's not about us.
BILLIE: Exactly. Your whole life is abstract. Your whole life is not about us. Do people have any kind of role in this life of yours—or is it all lamps? All ideas?

> ANNA *is shocked, says nothing.*

What about Edward, the husband? Did you spend so much time working out what was fair and just, what was criminal, that you never had any time for love? In all the judging—what have you won for yourself?
ANNA: You weren't there! You don't know anything about my life. You walk in here and start insulting me about a life you haven't even glimpsed.
BILLIE: No. Not even glimpsed.

> *Beat.*

If you don't acknowledge the mistakes you made, how can any of us move forward?
ANNA: If you don't acknowledge *your* history, how can we stop ourselves from falling backwards?
BILLIE: Fine. Fine then. Let's acknowledge my history, so that *I* don't have to fall backwards.

ANNA: Is this your revenge, Billie? Is that what this is?

BILLIE: [*all of a sudden, steely calm*] Do you think if I sought revenge, there would be a form of revenge good enough?

> *Beat.*

ANNA: Do you want an apology, is that it? Happily. I'll give it to you.

BILLIE: My name. Just say my name.

ANNA: I don't—

BILLIE: Just say my name.

ANNA: Billie.

BILLIE: Yes.

ANNA: Billie. Billie. Are you trying to make me feel—

BILLIE: What?

ANNA: Guilty?

BILLIE: *Do you*?

> *They stare at each other and then the moment breaks as* BILLIE *stands up and walks around the room.*

I fooled myself that you wanted to be found as much as I did.

ANNA: I wouldn't have agreed if I didn't. Of course I want this.

BILLIE: Really? Don't you mean of course you want to get *through* this? Civilised. Controlled. Managed.

ANNA: Look, I'm not sure what you're trying to—

BILLIE: What are we here for?

ANNA: To get to know each other.

BILLIE: But you don't want to know me! You want to deal with me.

ANNA: That's not true.

BILLIE: You've asked me *nothing* about my childhood. Aren't you interested?

ANNA: Of course I'm interested.

BILLIE: You never contacted them.

ANNA: No.

BILLIE: Did your husband want you to find me?

> *Beat.*

ANNA: Yes.

BILLIE: My ally.

ANNA: Don't do that!

BILLIE: Perhaps *he* understood what blood means! Perhaps he understood the difference. If I'd grown up with you, I could have fought and left and come back because *nothing* cancels out blood. Once I knew … living with them always felt dangerous. There was always the shadow of good manners involved. I couldn't walk away because there was nothing … biological to beckon me back. No safeguard of blood to say: We belong to each other no matter what. I thought you'd be so … hungry for me.

ANNA: Well …

BILLIE: That you would sit me down and feed me soup and tell me boring, comforting stories about your Amish quilts and you'd be so proud of me. Because I am successful. And I am attractive and slim and clever. And reasonable. And you would … hold me.

 Silence as they stare across the room at each other.

You're not my mother.

 ANNA *looks at her.*

Do you feel that way? Do you feel that there is a tremendous space there? Not social. Something, you know, down deep in the chromosomes, something so … crucial—that we cannot see it or name it.

 BILLIE *looks away.*

I will raise my children myself. So that when they are twenty-five, they won't be standing in strange living rooms, introducing themselves … I'm sorry if that upsets you.

ANNA: [*dawning on her just how malevolent* BILLIE *is*] No, you're not.

BILLIE: No. I'm not. I am what I have made of myself. I have dreams full of little children in tiny shoes. I dream the caramel smell of their soft skulls and their sweet see-through skin. And the children all have a particular expression in their eyes and when I catch a glimpse of myself in department store windows, I recognise it. Do you know what I dream of, Anna? I dream of myself.

ANNA: Look, Billie. Is this going to get us anywhere? What do you want me to do? What do you want from this?

BILLIE: You never wondered?

ANNA: Of course I did.

BILLIE: But …

ANNA: But I made another life. I closed my eyes. I switched off that part of myself.

BILLIE: How nice for you.

ANNA: Listen—it's hard for me too. You wanted this. I—I—I've had to get used to the idea. It's not easy for me either. We let go of a part of ourselves. And now the children are all coming back.

BILLIE: Do you seriously think this is a *rational* issue. Do you really think the *logical* response wins out here? Is that what you think? The writer husband—was he the keeper of the feelings?

ANNA: I don't think it's up to you to—

BILLIE: I think it *is* up to me. And I think I'm right … When he left, did you lose the keeper of the feelings? The one who got mad or sexy or jealous, so that you could maintain your fantastic equilibrium. Because it is fantastic, Anna. It is terrific.

ANNA: I feel things. [*Angrily*] You don't know anything about my marriage. *I felt things.*

BILLIE: [*heating up*] 'It's good to know you were in good hands.' As if you were leaving a child with a babysitter while you went to *Swan Lake*.

ANNA: [*really angry*] You have no right to tell me I have no feelings.

BILLIE: *Show* me.

ANNA: I can't display feelings on demand.

BILLIE: [*angry*] But you can display a *lack* of feeling on demand. When you give something away …

ANNA: There were reasons why I did what I did. There were reasons that I can't even put into words.

BILLIE: How nice for you to go to work watching life on film travel past you and just snipping out the bits you don't particularly like. What a lovely job. I bet you're brilliant at it.

ANNA: I was young.

BILLIE: Not as young as me.

ANNA: Have you had such a bad life?

BILLIE: No.

ANNA: You had things I couldn't have given you.

BILLIE: You had things I couldn't have got from anyone else! I tell you what 'women' need: the continuum. Our mother's mother, our mother, ourselves and our future in our children. Babies look up at their mother's faces and we glimpse our past and our future. We learn from them. Why we walk that way. Why we like cornflowers or rhubarb. Why we make bad choices or write good letters or dream a certain kind of dream.

Beat.

Your mother gave that to you. You took that away from me.

ANNA: Don't you think you're too old to blame?

BILLIE: My God, can't you hear anything without *judging* it?

ANNA: It's you, who's judging! Can't you see that? You're judging me for being a pitiful seventeen-year-old. You're judging me for a world that didn't look after *me*. Am I to blame for that? You're blaming the victim.

BILLIE: *I'm* the victim!

ANNA: Well, maybe we *both* are!

Pause.

BILLIE: If you were really so concerned about the world women inherited you would have held onto the one woman you brought into this world. You would have helped her inherit it.

Long silence. ANNA *takes in something of this: the anger gives way to a terrible sadness. She draws up words from within her brittle spirit, words which are causing her physical pain. She speaks gently, the surfaces shattered, real feeling at last emerging.*

ANNA: I didn't know what to do when Ed left. I wanted to be free. I thought I knew. It had to happen. But it felt as if my head had moved faster than my heart. I've been so skilled in taking all the facts and weighing them and making the right decision. You know, like a chemist. Like an alchemist. As if this thing inside me can be put in its place, this, this place where … where the feelings are kept.

Pause. Silent tears as she breaks.

Yes, I dreamt of you … I dreamt of a tiny baby crying in non-existent rooms. I climb out of my bed and walk through corridors searching for you and this terrible … this terrible realisation that I have had a child that I haven't been caring for, I have left it somewhere and forgotten it. And the dread! The loss … I have *longed* for you. For years I've lived in front of windows, catching glimpses of you through all the different parts of me. My heart. My head. My eyes. Sometimes just sensible thoughts: what school you're at. How tall you are. And then others ... others too ... Wondering what might have happened if I— And all the time, the knowledge that if I let go, I will lose myself. Like a giant wave that will fall over me and I will drown ...

> *She drops her hands.*

When I got your letter, I spent long hours thinking about a future I never thought I would have.

BILLIE: Tell me.

ANNA: I don't know. I don't know how.

BILLIE: Yes! Yes you do.

ANNA: Well ...

BILLIE: Tell me.

ANNA: Well, it's ...

BILLIE: It's a Sunday.

ANNA: Yes. You are living in a bright terrace house. It's painted ... Yellow.

BILLIE: And ...

ANNA: And I am standing at the front door and I ring the bell and inside I can see—

BILLIE: Shadows ...

ANNA: Moving ...

BILLIE: Yes ...

ANNA: And—I ...

BILLIE: Knock.

ANNA: Yes! The door opens and—

BILLIE: There is a child standing there.

ANNA: Yes. A child, smiling. I look at this child and it laughs and says—

> *Beat.*

BILLIE: Grandma.

> *Beat.*

ANNA: I hold the child and I walk in and the house is filled with sun and I give you two bunches of—

BILLIE: Blue irises.

Natasha Herbert as Billie in the 1993 Playbox Theatre Centre production. (Photo: Jeff Busby)

ANNA: And white—
BILLIE: Tulips.
ANNA: You are cooking. Something bubbles on the stove. I smell—
BILLIE: Nutmeg—
ANNA: I say: 'Billie'.
BILLIE: Yes.
ANNA: Did you—
BILLIE: Get the part—
ANNA: And you say—
BILLIE: Yes!
ANNA: And I—
BILLIE: Hold—
ANNA: You.
BILLIE: You—
ANNA: Hold—
BILLIE: Me.
ANNA: The child cries—
BILLIE: I turn, bend down—
ANNA: You sweep her up—
BILLIE: You turn to me and say—
ANNA: You need a haircut. Your hair is in your eyes.

> ANNA *walks up close to* BILLIE *and takes* BILLIE*'s head in her hands and looks into her face.*

Let me start again.

> *She stares at her face in silence.*

BILLIE: I—
ANNA: Yes—
BILLIE: I wish—
ANNA: Yes—Yes—
BILLIE: Can I—
ANNA: Yes. Yes—anything—
BILLIE: Sad. So—the sorrow—
ANNA: Which? Which?
BILLIE: At the—when I tried—
ANNA: Tried to—
BILLIE: Find—

ANNA: Find—
BILLIE: *You*— Find—
ANNA: Yes—
BILLIE: They told me—you were—
ANNA: Yes? Yes?
BILLIE: Dead—
ANNA: Me?
BILLIE: Dead—
ANNA: Me?
BILLIE: My mother. My—
ANNA: But I—
BILLIE: You see—
ANNA: I—
BILLIE: You see? You see—
ANNA: Your mother—
BILLIE: That was—
ANNA: They told you—
BILLIE: My mother—
ANNA: But I? I?
BILLIE: I went home—
ANNA: Yes—
BILLIE: I thought—
ANNA: Thought what? I don't—
BILLIE: My mother was dead. I had so much—
ANNA: My God—My—
BILLIE: *Grief*— As if—
ANNA: Go on—
BILLIE: I had lost all hope of—
ANNA: Of—
BILLIE: Catching up with myself. Feeling connected to—
ANNA: To the—
BILLIE: To the earth. And all I—I longed—I wished—all of it—
ANNA: Yes—
BILLIE: Was lost to me.

> *Beat.*

Do you see—
ANNA: But I'm—I'm *alive*—

BILLIE: You're alive. Yes. Yes.

> *Beat.*

I thought about all the daughters—
ANNA: Yes—
BILLIE: And all the mothers—
ANNA: Yes—
BILLIE: Drifting in their separate seas—
ANNA: Yes—Yes—
BILLIE: And how if only—
ANNA: Go on—
BILLIE: I might find—not—not—*my* mother but—
ANNA: What?
BILLIE: Another—
ANNA: Another?
BILLIE: Another mother. Whose child had not—
ANNA: [*confused*] I'm not—sorry—
BILLIE: Returned to her. Another mother.

> *Pause.* ANNA *tries to take this in.*

Stuart—he had access you see—to—
ANNA: You're—you're (saying)—
BILLIE: Records. And found for me—
ANNA: Wait—
BILLIE: A woman who—
ANNA: A woman—
BILLIE: Who gave birth to—
ANNA: A woman—
BILLIE: A daughter on the same—
ANNA: Wait—
BILLIE: Day. You see? The fences that keep thoughts neat and orderly just—
ANNA: Wait. Wait—
BILLIE: Came down. And I was— The *sweetness*—
ANNA: You're saying—
BILLIE: The sweetness of the thought—of that embrace—
ANNA: You.

> *Beat.*

You.

Beat.

You dreamt this up?

BILLIE: I—

ANNA: You dreamt this up? You—

Pause as ANNA *absorbs what has been revealed.*

BILLIE: It seemed so—

ANNA: So—

BILLIE: The chance was there—for—

ANNA: For *you*—

BILLIE: For both of us!—

ANNA: This—cruelty—

BILLIE: A gift—

ANNA: This cruelty—this—

BILLIE: A gift for both—

ANNA: For me?

BILLIE: A gift of—

ANNA: Of what?

BILLIE: Of resolution.

Beat.

That's why—

ANNA: You're not—

BILLIE: That's why I'm—

ANNA: You're not my—

BILLIE: That's why I'm here—

ANNA: [*dawning on her*] Then who?

BILLIE: No—

ANNA: Then where is my—

BILLIE: *I'm* here. That's why—

ANNA: My God—You gave her to me—

BILLIE: Yes—

ANNA: You gave her and you—

BILLIE: No— No—

ANNA: You *take* her!

Beat.

Still—

BILLIE: Still I'm—
ANNA: Still born.

> *Pause.*

I started to … Do you realise … I started to—*love*—
BILLIE: Yes—
ANNA: I started to feel as if I could—
BILLIE: Yes—You can—you can—with me—
ANNA: As if I was—melting—
BILLIE: Yes—I gave you—
ANNA: You're killing me—
BILLIE: No! No!
ANNA: I was all right!—
BILLIE: No—
ANNA: I was all right and then you—
BILLIE: I've—
ANNA: You've murdered me …
BILLIE: We can— You see— We *can*—I've—
ANNA: What are you? What?
BILLIE: *Given* you—
ANNA: I started to—
BILLIE: Something—
ANNA: I started to—love … You felt that?
BILLIE: Yes—Yes!
ANNA: And then you? My God … My God …

> *Beat.*

BILLIE: Does it— Listen to me, Anna— Does it—
ANNA: Does it?
BILLIE: Matter? Does it—
ANNA: What?
BILLIE: Whose daughter I am—
ANNA: What? What did you—
BILLIE: Whose mother you—
ANNA: I'm not—
BILLIE: No. No.
ANNA: I'm not your—

> *Beat.*

BILLIE: You could have been.

Beat.

ANNA: You took away my peace—
BILLIE: No!
ANNA: My house. My peace—
BILLIE: No! No!
ANNA: I have—
BILLIE: You have—
ANNA: Nothing. Left. I have—
BILLIE: Me. You have me. You have—

Blackout.

Silence.

The light comes up on a new ANNA—bright almost cheerful, compared to the devastated ANNA we have left. There is a sense that time has passed.

ANNA: [*to the audience*] I gave away the furniture. I rang the Brotherhood, actually. Someone, somewhere in a housing commission flat has my Philippe Starck lamp. I bought every cleaning agent on the market and I scrubbed my white house until I had to wear sunglasses just to sit in it. I stayed in the empty clean house for three weeks. And then, so strange, one afternoon I was lying on my couch staring at a small insect that had landed on my Kundera novel and I felt her unmistakable presence.

Beat. BILLIE and ANNA are present, but separate, facing the audience.

BILLIE: I call to her—
ANNA: She calls to me—
BILLIE: She answers me—
ANNA: She finds me—
BILLIE: She likes the way I look—
ANNA: She's beautiful—
BILLIE: She's proud of me—
ANNA: She knows how hard it was for me. She feels my pain—
BILLIE: I tell her I'm an actress and she rings up all her friends to tell them. She makes me dinner and we drink wine.

ANNA: We drink wine and talk for days. I really like her. She's so strong and full of life.

BILLIE: She regrets. She has wept for me.

ANNA: And sweetly, so softly, we weep together for all the problems and the grief. And later, we go to the movies ...

Blackout.

THE END

*Sue Ingleton (left) as Anna and Natasha Herbert as Billie in the
1993 Playbox Theatre Centre production. (Photo: Jeff Busby)*

Other plays by Joanna Murray-Smith and available from Currency Press

SWITZERLAND

It's 1995 in the Swiss Alps and the ailing reclusive crime writer Patricia Highsmith is visited by a young man from her publisher, sent to convince her to write the final instalment of her best-selling *Mr Ripley* series. What first appears to be a standard cat-and-mouse game of wit and wiles, soon becomes a dance to the death. Who is the cat and who is the mouse? And … who will make it out of Switzerland alive?

ISBN 978 1 92500 556 1

HONOUR

What happens when everything you have used to define yourself—every quality, role and affiliation—suddenly abandon you? What happens when a mature, intelligent, responsible and loving woman finds her life disappearing?

ISBN 978 0 86819 782 1

NIGHTFALL

It's twilight, and a mother and father wait for the promised return of their daughter who vanished ten years earlier. A stranger arrives at their doorstep, warning them that their daughter will only return on certain agonising terms.

ISBN 978 0 86819 919 1

RAPTURE

A vivid play set among intelligent and educated people whose cynicism appears to answer all questions and who navigate uncertainty with ease. What could possibly shock or unsettle them? When two of their number claim to have found God, the consequences are profound. Ethics and certainties are tested on a battleground of inexplicable belief.

ISBN 978 0 86819 679 4

BOMBSHELLS

Six monologues made famous by actress Caroline O'Connor, exposing six women balancing their inner and outer lives with humour and often desperate cunning. They range in age from a feisty teenager to a 64-year-old widow yearning for the unexpected.

ISBN 978 0 86819 751 7

THE FEMALE OF THE SPECIES

Thirty years ago Margot Mason, pioneer of the Women's Liberation movement and fearless academic, wrote her groundbreaking work. Now she is faced with Molly, an unannounced visitor who produces a gun and calmly informs Margot that she intends to kill her because she blames her for warping her mother's mind and ruining her life with her hit book *The Cerebral Vagina*.

ISBN 978 0 86819 825 5

NINETY

It is no use, but William gives Isobel ninety minutes anyway. They were once married—and now Isabel just wants ninety minutes. Soon William will be married again, so ninety is all she has to make her case. Ninety to remember what they had. Ninety to regain what was lost. Just ninety minutes to rediscover love or call it a day, forever.

ISBN 978 0 86819 851 4

ROCKABYE

Sidney can feel her career slipping down the plughole. No one loves a pop star when she's forty—not if she isn't Madonna or Kylie. So unless she wants to join the ranks of the has-beens on the casino circuit, she'd better get herself a hit. But what if she regains the whole world and still feels that something's missing?

ISBN 978 0 86819 860 6

SONGS FOR NOBODIES

When a great singer lets her voice float out over the anonymous crowd, or form the grooves of thousands of records, or flow through radios into millions of homes across the world, she makes countless unknown connections with people. In *Songs for Nobodies*, we meet five unknown women who are touched by the great singers seen to be living the dream: Judy Garland, Patsy Cline, Edith Piaf, Billie Holiday and Maria Callas. Five great singers, five monologues.

ISBN 978 0 86819 893 4

THE GIFT

Sadie and Ed meet Martin and Chloë at a holiday resort and instantly hit it off, despite coming from completely different worlds. When Martin saves Ed's life, everyone knows the debt can never be properly repaid. But Ed is rich and Chloë and Martin have a need so great it seems divine providence when Ed, wanting to show his gratitude, gives the young couple a year to decide on an appropriate gift. Yet when the year is up, surely Chloë and Martin's wish is something no-one could possibly grant?

ISBN 978 0 86819 915 3

STORIES OF LOVE AND DECEPTION

An anthology of three plays, *Stories of Love and Deception* is a keenly engaging discussion of our most dearly-held values and their ramifications. This trilogy includes *Day One, a Hotel, Evening*; *True Minds*; and *Fury*.

ISBN 978 1 92500 530 1

www.currency.com.au

Visit Currency Press' website now to:

- Buy your books online
- Browse through our full list of titles, from plays to screenplays, books on theatre, film and music, and more
- Choose a play for your school or amateur performance group by cast size and gender
- Obtain information about performance rights
- Find out about theatre productions and other performing arts news across Australia
- For students, read our study guides
- For teachers, access syllabus and other relevant information
- Sign up for our email newsletter

The performing arts publisher